Misapprehensions

BY E. A. MARKHAM

Poetry

Human Rites
Anvil, 1984

Lambchops in Papua New Guinea
IPNGS, 1985

Living in Disguise
Anvil, 1986

Towards the End of a Century
Anvil, 1989

Letter from Ulster & The Hugo Poems
Littlewood Arc, 1993

Stories

Something Unusual
Ambit Books, 1986

Ten Stories
Pavic, 1994

Travel

A Papua New Guinea Sojourn: More Pleasures of Exile
Carcanet, 1996

Editor

Merely a Matter of Colour
with Arnold Kingston
'Q' Books, 1973

Hugo Versus Montserrat
with Howard A. Fergus
Linda Lee Books, 1989

Hinterland
Caribbean Poetry from the West Indies & Britain
Bloodaxe, 1989

The Penguin Book of Caribbean Short Stories
1996

E. A. MARKHAM

Misapprehensions

[signature] 14.10.95

ANVIL PRESS POETRY

Published in 1995
by Anvil Press Poetry Ltd
69 King George Street London SE10 8PX

This book is published
with financial assistance from
The Arts Council of England

Designed and composed by Anvil
Photoset in Plantin by Typestream
Printed and bound in England
by Morganprint (Blackheath) Ltd
Distributed by Password, Manchester

ISBN 0 85646 271 3

ACKNOWLEDGEMENTS

Versions of some of these poems have appeared in the
following magazines, journals and newspapers: *Ambit, London
Quarterly, New Statesman & Society,* the British Council's
*New Writing 4, The North, Outposts, Poetry Durham, Poetry
Ireland Review, Poetry London Newsletter, Poetry Review, The
Rialto, Sheffield Thursday, Stand, The Sunday Gleaner*
(Jamaica), *The Sunday Times* and the *Trinidad & Tobago
Review.* 'Bosnia, Rwanda' has been read on BBC radio. Of
the prose, 'Life Before the Revolution' first appeared in
London Magazine, and 'The Gift' in *The Rialto.*

Contents

VIII

*When seagulls follow a trawler, it is because they think
sardines will be thrown into the sea*
— ERIC CANTONA

*Culture is what permits a butcher
to call 'himself' a doctor*
— AN AMERICAN AT A CONFERENCE

I

A Death in the Family

i.m. Andrew Salkey, 1928–1995

Dear Andrew, I heard of your passing in passing,
tipping it a little in the flow of loss we must wade through
and I apologize, as we do, for not being there;
we expected you back, not like this, to those interrupted
talks in Moscow Road, which would go better now
with the strain of travel and search for allies behind us; we'd be
    wiser
now – all those Jerusalems desecrated – glossing friendship
with no sparring for advantage, no fear of surrender.

You signed off your letters, *Venceremos*. I'd planned to answer
the last one with a quip, a bit of gossip, tales
of our slippage over here. Forgive me if this sounds like a voice
grown distant; but thank you, Andrew Salkey, anthologist of wastes
and triumphs of our story. Ever frail but renewable, our barrier
against spoilers who make the earth more wretched, holds your
    text.

II

From Crouch End
to Highgate

April the 28th Street

Thinking of your birthday

That way, as not to tempt fate, they pass it off
as an address. And you know how it is
with these entries in the diary, mentions
on the radio that arrest you for a minute,
as you picture a small battle fought in some distant
language, hot young men and women straggling towards the
    Capital,
now fêted by strangers hazy about their names,
or what they looked like, or whom they loved.

In time the street is a public square flagged
for celebration, and I, through special privilege
of the unpartnered, am transported there, re-admitted
before its gel into history, its run to ritual,
urging life back into one April partner:
and here, alone in this room, celebrate her birth.

A Diary Entry Not For Publication

So, this is day one of the life.
Off-stage, I've fought off grizzly bears
who once soiled her bed: all disreputable
ancestors will stay banished.
So, our introduction outside history
takes up years of the life.
And we survive all that. Back together,
I own up to maleness and assume the rota of men in her life.

Phew! I'm her man, her woman and something else.
Ancestors in the bathroom mirror
smudge another face till I'm grizzly
at her crying. But washed and brushed, pre-this, post-that
we return to day one of the life;
though this time round you must imagine her voice.

Reprieve

Guilty as charged: take away the bruise
on that face, humiliation by commission
on another. Add such lies of omission
as come to mind. Too smug, too smug to choose
this way out: I did in one house when we were young
ignore a cry – like spilt wine on the pavement – and read on.
     Substitute
this house for that, and a man not destitute
of imagination who stole ten years from a woman.

For reprieve I say: since then I've tracked
down part of *A la Recherche* . . . missing
from her library. So let me hurry back
upstairs (past the Guermantes' drawing-room lot) to
prevent a bruise. First, the hugs and kissing.
Then, years of putting wine back into her bottle.

16

These Foolish Things . . .

With you it's spring, always, in the desert,
autumn anywhere for those grown ripe
with spring; herbs of Provence in our garden
in Highgate; Basmati rice cooked just so;
nation-language: *bwoy, wha' chuppetness you talkin'?*
And maybe Louis Armstrong and Piaf for singing
telegram . . . and is that Desmond Tutu dancing the night away?
These foolish things remind me of you.

Without you, colour shrugged off the trees.
Spices from the cupboard running out
without protest. The duets mimed by extras
on the evening News show us writ large, show us grown small.
Basmati rice burnt: *bwoy, dis is no joke, eh!*
So . . . *these foolish things . . .*

At Paul and Deirdre's, Dublin

I'm not the warm knife exxing through
your butter . . . My mantra: I'm not the warm knife . . .

And now I think of lunch with friends pleased
to talk of healing things, discovering
new plants in the garden when a guest
arrives with a story she wants to tell.
But she, like you, will yield to prior
claims of garden, and promise her story with the sweet.

New thoughts of knife and butter,
and our own escape from the worst that might happen;
and wine and dinner and children served,
and everyone says yes please, let's have the sweet –
which is magical, like something tropical in the garden.
Like your pruned storybeds, sprouting again.

In Place of Heirlooms

for Mimi

Yellow mugs and cupboards that refashioned
one kitchen into another, twinning our space,
large red cushions of balloons, ships, flying-carpets – discarded
    now
by others as clutter – and that's not the start of it.
So pick it up in the middle of the story,
past the accidents of geology and men's wars,
and migrations which baffle the mind's logic
as if we were issue of some Biblical farmer's seed:

blessèd the day at Totleigh with you in polka-dots,
and a challenge that was young for us, panic-babble silenced;
and an itch on the skin assuaged by laying on of hands,
and the promise of seagrapes and hummous and sugarapple and
    rosewater
to irrigate, yes, this patch of desert, to open up that dungeon,
and – still in the middle of the story – time for tears; and poetry.

Turkey

That's us in Turkey with the children.
That's the family that might have been.
Who has a right to this memory, these lyric skies?
In Turkey our worlds met: East playing host
to a West you suspect of converting me.
We could live here, walking to the village
for water, food, the dust not showing up on postcards:
a villa near Fethiye, olives, yogurt etc. for lunch.

And now the villa built and lived in. Ah.
Sometimes at night I wake to Allan Poe sweat
at secrets entombed in the bedroom wall: the black cat,
screeching curses, for you, telegenic in new company.
How then to serve this sentence to life without superstition,
only memory, and a chain of logic on the imagination?

The Return

a

He's thinking squalls & troughs, etc.,
of people crossing red seas, deep seas,
of having at last ground to defend.
I'm cold and brutal (she will dismiss this)
not by choice, but because love translates badly
in this or that language forced on family
where every member speaks with an accent:
how to correct this

was on no course of study, no National Health
agenda. Here he is again looming,
part of the landscape. She's thinking: I've got legs,
arms, faculties: why continue to circle
this little island to find port? It's a desert
without the records. Her luxury, the tongue of a sailor.

b

And *he's* thinking of large issues;
of peoples recrossing the centuries,
of blood like ketchup, the leader held aloft.

Or even, trying to get it right
in the head: that conference in Paris
where he read a Paper

more difficult than it seemed; his typewriter,
broken in transit, hinting at something.

She's thinking: it was with him, here,
half a life ago I tried to imagine
his father as part of the future;
and of the night we watched a young weatherman
on television, looking like no man that age should;
and here is Michael Fish again, surviving the weather.

Taxis

And you know some things seem to be passed down
through the family, like being in the army
or claiming a favourite grandmother's illness:
they say, once, the ruler of a country instead of killing
people, like his father, made an enemy of the flowers;
the smell upset him. When the country was rid of blooms
he discovered what made him nauseous was new paint
applied whenever he visited a school or factory.

But taxis were the things to bring tears
to our eyes. When her first driver smiled
and he had bad teeth, she felt cheated,
like flying to America in a second class train
with waitress service. The last time she cried in a taxi
was the night a man wanted to share, and she said no.

A Story

*Angela Carter was asked for an example of a modern fairy
tale. And she said: think of a King visiting another King
in the middle of the night, to ask for a cup of sugar . . .*

King Castine knocks on Stapleton's
door late at night for a cup of sugar.
Come in, says Stapleton: what magic
brings you to my door on the one night
in 500 years I find myself at home?
I'm King of St Caesare and know
these things by inheritance, says Castine.
Or by lottery of being King for tonight.

This is very interesting, says Stapleton:
what does it feel like being King for the night?
It feels incomplete without the sugar.
And what is sugar, pray, is it your Queen?
Yes, she is the quest of 500 years, the door
that opens when you knock. Interesting, says Stapleton.

Stable Doors and All That

So, talk of your little *self*
till they despair, one after the other, give up
and turn away to breathe new air.
Now, say the prayer for things lost:
on the one hand vanity, on the other
the mirage of life. In contrition
revisit a house (alas) disused;
here's the garden between birth and burial-place:

CASTINE: a priest-like figure in exile from the island, claiming
legitimacy from a pre-Columbian past.

feelgood? feelbad?
Say someone spares a thought, thinks:
maybe he won't push now we're off the edge!
To prove them all wrong he comes
laden with goodies the lady craves,
setting up stall where there is no custom.

Stand-In

They spent decades tracking the children:
not much to go by, no names, a hint only of the parents
when young. They lost heart when the serial novel
of refugees threw up a happy episode on the news. Each relived
the other's life, visiting old haunts, pondering
partners that might have been. The fun of it –
as with all addiction – was knowing you could give it up
if you tried. And then one day they gave it up.

And they would celebrate the things not gone missing
in their lives, and not resent the sight of twosomes *everywhere*
settling for second best, in time doing better
than they feared (ha!) – their narratives more readable now.
So it's not the same when he fumbles the stand-in
and she remembers him as someone else.

Roses

The smell won't go away: roses, he says, roses;
and moves house and country to settle
in the South of France: this workman's cottage
will grow to respect a small ambition:
villa, pond clearing into pool, the gardener
sprigging *fosse septique* with perfumes
of the region. Visitors leave restored
hearty with the whiff of what escapes

somewhat like a woman far from the scene who, yes, curses
the unguarded moment, untenses, doesn't quite flush you
out of mind: there you are doing good works
somewhere, VSOing, losing yourself in frenzy.
It won't work, she knows, seeking to atone, to justify.
Oh, there you are again, self-renewing, sniffing roses!

But

But I'm careful to go with the rhythm, to show
willing, to fall on my face. But you know that.
So let me relearn your scales, flow with the music.
Though I don't dance. And this is not about dancing.
Though I must adjust, shift position.
But darling, think of it: if the ball's out of court
you win the game. Not that this is about
winning points or playing tennis!

You're out of tune with instruments of the house,
the family: jokes about metronome ring false.
I'm the woman serving at tennis while you ache
to smash the winner: you batter me with buts.

Yes. And here's another lob of 'sorry' you must decline. But
why not play that other game with no rules, just ifs and buts!

24

Oh, That Poem About Bosnia

X, from a distance, writes a poem on occasion of your burnt
arm, making Y, the lover, jealous. The mark, not a scar,
unlike its neighbours fading with neglect, earns more than a shrug
when glanced at. It's not love, of course (a rabbit
bouncing away from danger in an urban forest; a hedgehog
escaping tyres) but reminders of, well, pre-war times. The lover,
late to spot the disfigurement, makes up for lost time with lines
that plunge you into something worse than a kitchen; your scar a
    symbol

of things gone wrong. These men conduct the lovefight over a
    woman's
blemish – who has a right to it, whose caring
is persuasive, who got in first: there's a history there.
OK: this isn't the domestic mark that all women carry.
There's still a whiff of burning, she says to the newmen puffing
out bushfires, condemning mass rape and genocide; I'm home.

Love and Death

Poets, seeming to protest too much, write
last, last poems to loved ones;
and how can I say this isn't happening when,
as now, I can't keep separate converging
lines of loss – *this is mine*; *this is ours*.
That afternoon at an event I walked in
without you, stripped of meaning, and joined them
commemorating the death of a friend.

And here we were, at least, growing older
with grace, one fewer on the platform
than announced. And when we stood for a minute
in remembrance, I used that trust and tried
to remagic us back in place when the world
was busy, and people not like us mourned the dead.

III

Family

Mother

What right have we to her memories,
'La Contessa' painted thirty years ago
by the fake Italian to preserve the house
through the family's, quote, wintering: there'd be no return
for her but to lie with ancestors where *we* won't follow.
And the resentments, for loss of her spaces,
for imprisonment in the Kingdom of her sons –
Zanussi refrigerator notwithstanding: who will claim the credit?

And now with the prod of a partner
you must impress, you are tempted to remove
that other mask, for the face underneath is primed
to speak those things that trouble us, as silence must now
mean silencing. And would Italian classes have helped?
And had she plans to kill us and escape?

Mammie Columbus

He shouldn't drink wine or gargle with a cold
and traumatize the throat-muscles: doctor
follows his mother's advice even though
she hasn't read, well, Kling's *A Brief History
of Finland*. But a tussle's on for the rôle
of pioneer in this house: you shrug off
names that ash you like dandruff, toying with you.
Mammie won't now lament journeys which failed
to discover treasure in family
preachers and teachers, this one a doctor,
but not of patients. In uniform old times
might mock, she masters the digital
laundrette and a machine that scrambles eggs.
She's Columbus. Scientist. Sibelius.

Drawing-rooms

i

Yet, you can be human in this place, with new rules:
so make the best of it; wash, clean and prepare
yourself for the 'drawing-room' as if nothing happened.
They seem so clever, sons, knowing how the world
works, knowing why drawing-rooms can't be transported
like necessary luggage; they point at this or that Minister
getting it wrong, talking of governments now, not the Church;
while a daughter hints of curse put on women of this house.

With marriage left behind she imagines new guests
invited to tea; they're forgiving, while sons
who are not architects and magicians plan to feed
a world howling on TV. Time yet to lie in style
drawing hush from visitors: at her daughter's the sermon
is dreaming of salads instead of meat. And she is no Pharisee.

ii

An old Sunday, she said, if that could be arranged,
in her drawing-room with friends; for what's the use
of dresses she had no place to wear, or presents
she'd pass on from children too grown-up and distracted
to know what she might like: they talk her into
things that dazzle and reflect, they don't wish to be cruel
with these bigger gifts than she deserves.
(And should she be punished, still, for noting this?)

So that year she asked for the old drawing-room
with Sunday visitors and conversation of how the house
sheltered dozens during the hurricanes of '24 & '28;
or a glimpse of her mother's coffin lodged there for an hour
to remind us that those who died had their rights –
like the boy-men still arguing difference between flowers and
    weeds.

Conversations at Upton Park *i*

Says the boy come to visit his mother: Ruby
was the horse and the rabbits didn't have names.
But she knew that, knows that. Loss
of memory didn't extend to things at home.
Though thirty years and more of changing shape
confused children with parents; and who knows
what's embarrassing when a boy with white hair
and his mother confess over a cup of tea?

So they would keep this amongst themselves:
if suffering was done these days on television,
some things not seen must be safe. And Ruby
and the rabbits may not have understood pain.
Yet, when he went on those trips and couldn't write, she glimpsed
his ghost, sometimes, on the television and had nightmares.

Conversations at Upton Park *ii*

The father they understood; men were like that,
though father was younger than this son now
who couldn't be believed: would the boy need
more years to grow into his inheritance?
So they talked about his brother, grown up too soon,
and out of their lives: he had been wounded, pioneering
for the family, fought a long battle for compensation
which went to his head. Of course, they called him 'Skiver'.

All sorts of things bring this back:
the way one son grows into another denying
a gap in the family, still holding out
for an award lost in the post; the way no one remembers
how all this started – with a boy
giving three fingers to the machine, a skiver that sliced leather.

The New Stapleton Will

They're still fighting over the legacy.
He remembers a gathering of the clan, in-laws,
he alone partnerless: they aren't curious
about contents of a will where things,
as always in the family, divide equally:
a share in the house, bits of land in a place
not lived – an anchor
allowing the family boat to drift without panic.

First, to those who stay married:
for such breadth of generosity, a reward.
Then muscles tense to hear how the anointed son
is to be privileged. After loving preamble, yes, he inherits
his share and more, if he brings no long-legged, long-haired
second wife into the house. *Amen*, says someone who isn't a
     preacher.

Stapleton: The Dialogues

i

HIM (*still in debt, but . . .*)

                   These things have I done since you ceased
to be impressed. I have refashioned the portrait
of someone you might like who denounced me as fraud,
giving her the good lines, no jokes
at her expense (still eating meat, though) I have
in the laundrette instructed a young woman, a stranger,
in use of the machines; now I've owned up to an incident
– in China? – that no one else has (and I've escaped the pride of
    surgeons).

HER

Boy (you saying your prayers?) how come you still talking to me
as if I'm someone else; I feel shame that nothing
change with you (no wife, no children to distract you
from foolishness, *and you still going to laundrette?*) Praise
the Lord about the surgeons. But where's the woman in China
who going let you snore at night, instead of talking to the dead?

35

You're older than Lenin by *months* and *looks*
and arrogant as the head of who knows what? (excuse
my useless information, it fills the time); you've changed
name into initials in preparation for leadership;
we've given you space, let you off birthdays, hospital
visits, the small-talk of lives – like the courtesy
of matching a face to a name outside your interest;
we show tolerance of your living spaces, the still-life
of books and papers shorn of distraction;
your scorn of doctors and lawyers from home etc. made us
nerve ourselves for something special. And still, everywhere,
people looking like us are used to advertise despair:
a world of casualty, war without end, humiliation –
that's where we live. And we did trust you. So what is to be done?

A History

1956. A daughter. Conceived
the day you returned £1 to the girl
at the post office. Excess change. Her blush,
not quite champagne was a sip of something Cyprusy
as if the entrails of dead sheep and cattle
showed this house, long built on nuance,
its turn of luck. A father fearing brick
and bottle in the street, talked up futures.

Now, a woman of years unbelieving
omens. Prohibitions of dad return
faith to clay. And she's released
into life on a wing and a prayer.
Pundits pundit. Crows come to Bosnia.
Cuito. 1993. Bodies, bodies everywhere.

Colour

Liberty in Ladbroke Grove. Someone films
her, pins her to the wall. Ethnic.
But here there's no blood on the floor,
the place cleaned up, walls papered over,
fresh paint. Pity about the locks.
New name on letters now, Ms Liberty, daughter
of the house, not the one murdered in her bed.
Though the house still bears a grudge.

Liberty, flagship of a family
will sail clear of danger. On clean sheets,
smelling the sea, her mother dies without violence.
That's to come. Here, she lays ghosts, regains the street
as nasties from the woodwork mingle with the crowd.
This is a film. To be continued.

That Day or Another

A dad for the day, he tells the story of the bank
plunged into excitement of power-cut
and no one pulling a gun, customers third world and calm:
she thinks of hospitals and emergency generators,
she thinks her children must not be orphaned;
she listens to the joke only dads are allowed to make
in public, and fails to protect her life from ridicule:
she won't be accused of lacking humour.

A holiday for jokes and normality to be paid for
later: the family play a game of other families;
the children, on the warpath, speak out of the side
of their mouth; the dad for the day tells a story of power-cuts
and emergency generators gunning the hospital lights.
It feels odd, somehow, playing Bonnie to Pewter tonight.

Suspended

Good times, bad times. They danced,
love hard against love, expiring on the stairs
as if scoring at football without the frenzy. Good times.
Bad times. On her back laid low, a row
about men and women. Fun to watch the box from a rigged
mirror – he imagining great ladies
of another age. She? Pain and subtitles
the wrong way round to be argued later.

And now that the back is all but mended,
now the game's been un-suspended,
this or that act once more defended,
yes, now that the rift is all but ended,
the crowd, referee, the TV all so splendid –
who cares that today's turf is less well-tended!

Second Thoughts on Andrew

i.m. Andrew Salkey, 1928–1995

On the bus, thinking of some minor form of advancement,
I acknowledged her, not quite like us, head-wrapped
in religious imagery, urging a daughter's shoe
back from my seat. *Thank you, Lady*, edging towards us.
And I slid back to dreamland, worrying a nose with the back
of my hand; and here she is again – face filled in
under the veil – holding out tissue to save me from loutishness:
a public kindness the like to bring on guilt.

I was not using the back of my hand as handkerchief,
I say to absent mother, grandmother who still make me confess;
I was not disgracing you in public. And then you shimmered
into view, reacting with less baggage to this kindness
from a stranger extending the shape of family: *recognize it.*
By so much, today, are we enlarged, and I'm reporting back to you.

IV

Bits of History

Sketch

O, I know what makes the gaze wander
from this feast, a Van Dyck beauty brought up
to date with small-screen countenance, not younger
than present company – too shrewd for that – but

bilingual: how she mouths it, one tongue
for public fare, the other less than cute
for present munching. Tough-minded and pliant. So move along
mere mortal. And there she is, stepping out of Beirut!

Out of Beirut, Bosnia, Cuito . . .
And this paragon must stay sane,
and turn from traps that hopefuls lay at her feet. Oh,
and distrust scented gardens, rivers cleansed in her name,
and rhyming dictionaries with lovewords, godwords, words to raise
     the dead
– for what? To embrace you, blind, deaf, ugly, prosefarting in her
     bed?

Wounded

A specimen in decline who'll never whistle
through perfect teeth again; and takes the fight
to dentists of the world – and others
who make him blind and deaf and lethal
about bank managers. But face to face
he laughs them into sympathy: with faithless
wives (for they are men) and daughters
recruited to the enemy . . . ah, why kick a lame dog?

But *here* the warrior cuts from her nails
knives and sharpened things; traps in her mouth
scalding water from her tongue, till it's safe,
like lovejuice, to swallow or spit out.
And again, till she's spent, can do no harm to this husk of man
demanding love from a woman in her prime.

Identity Parade

They pulled him in because of the gun,
the mask, the moneybag. Volunteers
behind the grille replay the scene in the bank.
They're street-wise: should he escape with money
the state will fall. *He's familiar enough to us.*
What price a mistake on the streets of London,
of Rio? This eye-witness takes a closer look,
lifts the mask, fingers the gun

keeps going to show how it's done.
There's no doubt he's the man, she knows
him from elsewhere. But disarmed, couldn't he be put
to the use a girl always wanted? He's game and naked,
moves to mug her; and what she did then
confirms a rumour gaining ground.

44

Hostages

At the end of the line (painful phrase
so stick to trains) handcuffed and waiting . . .
Get off at an early station and take them with you.
Your sex is holstered, is exposed
and makes them do your bidding: the world
will agree they had no choice but to obey
a man so armed – and with a stocking, too, over his head!

The defence will bluff: *All men are primed
to go off*. So many fine chaps wearing stockings!
This one rides his space-train, two extra
tickets – seat either side – in his gift. He tempts
strap-hangers to relax. But they, too long oppressed –
the state, the world, the next few hours –

panic at this kindness; demand something worse.

Rescue

I've been to a hundred and sixty-nine countries,
my daughter claims 3,000 books in her room,
and when the bombs came falling down and we had to leave home
without packing a suitcase, without a change of clothes,
with no one to give us safe passage and passports
so that some lost at sea were soon forgotten
(and even the sea, they say, is now bad land)
we passed the message to anyone who would listen

which in some translation goes like this:
I've been to 169 countries, my daughter has 30,000 books
in her head; the grave of a cousin, though not found, is decorated;
the war's on, we're in exile, not waiting for rescue
but checking sea and land for survivors (hard-bodied, winged and
        literate)
to inherit my travel, my daughter's books, like old family.

Yugoslavia

She knew it for the wine even though
they spelt it differently. And now
they say the country is no more.
She's resigned to it, things moving fast
to upstage and make her foolish.
She can't blame parents, school or lovers
pulling her the wrong pace along the world.
And here she is, too late for Yugoslavia.

And she goes to the bin from last night
and finds a switch of label
on a bottle she enjoyed: she's caught out
by these games. Or has she been drinking Bulgaria
all along? Well then, hang on to this. Stay ahead.
The labels read like films. She likes the Djuigerov.

Bosnia, Rwanda

You may find some scenes of this report distressing.
My friend in the garden puffs at a cigarette
not allowed in the house: though the air is already
smoke-stained, we must think that small things matter.
I look down from the window, calm as a Prime Minister
re-shuffling the pack: familiar birds and rabbits
roar into action elsewhere. So let us talk of the dentist,
the doctor insensitive to our needs; and apologize to absent
        children.

And who knows if dinner is late because of a health warning,
or if talk, like a car vandalized in the carpark, will get us going?
Round the table old partners come together in the shuffle
and someone in from the garden lights up our tolerance.
The world does its worst off our screen while we turn wine
back into water. Now whisper it: *don't we find this reassuring!*

DJUIGEROV: a Bulgarian film-maker.

Dispatch to Mammie on Mandela's Election

In gratitude, in suspicion, we tend not to write
the happy marriage, as the cry of de-coupling vies
with colonies migrating to aid. (Talking over distance
affects my voice, but I imagine we'd be kinder to you, now,
with grapes and cricket from the Cape.)
We consigned rogue governments and lucifers
of industry to the pulpit hell they liked too well:
they laughed at us. And, yes, Mandela's children have voted.

Dear Mammie, through us, you're alive to see it.
And friends ask after you, late for the party.
We've cleared the basement space for who knows what?
No shrine to young woman murdered on doorstep in Surrey;
no court for boys attacking the morning train from Aberdeen.
We're neither free nor fair. Still, night follows day where we live.

A Secret Ceremony

As expected there's dissension in the ranks;
Those who talk up futures note the sign
As fugitives and molesters of the weak and unlucky
Point the finger at other household names
Unapologetic and mythic: this is our congregation
Charged to out-hymn one another.

And the Big Man in the village speaks for us;
For our space is limited, we live on an island.
For we live on an island our backs to the sea,
A ring of water, wreckage and dead fish around us.
Our parents welcomed to this island, turned
Desperadoes into household names: this is
Our history, our geography; we must survive it
Without force of arms. Let me show you how.

2020

And the family plot here is larger
than its parent in St Caesare – a shift
to where we belong. Yet they ask again:
And where're you from? masking threats you ignore.
We've gone through the barrier of anger,
and this generation holds its elders
to account. Hurdles cleared in sport and art,
even learning, are coloured air and space.

And here we are once more perhaps saying grace
before dinner, grateful that this or that
whispering disease hasn't found us out.
As the star, I light tunnels of distrust.
Some make jokes about my hair which grows in a TV
ad: who would guess we could still do that!

V

Some Extended Footnotes

i.m. Linda Ann Eliza Lee Markham
1913–1989

Life Before the Revolution

That was what we used to call it, *Life Before the Revolution*, and we used, in the early days, to draw improbable parallels between us and the victims of real revolutions who had to flee abroad, leaving their possessions behind. And we would volunteer a member of the family dying heroically in the revolution – a grand uncle, maybe, or a dad; or even the headstrong twin-brother who was all the things I wasn't. But that game grew stale and 'Life Before the Revolution' was clung to only by my mother, who summoned it when the family got together and she wished to recall the old days, to reflect on her properties, her houses, her five houses, which were too vast and precious to pack up and bring with us to England, in 1956. We would still try to forestall her, to make a joke of it, of the packing up and bringing of land as well as houses – for even her famous trunk didn't have room enough for that: and how would you get it all to fit on that little Italian boat?

'It wasn't a little boat!' She was indignant at the thought that she had come here on a *little* boat, much more so than the fact that she had been sea-sick on the three-week voyage, because that was a personal frailty and had nothing to do with her status on the island (and, by implication, her reception in this country). But it was good to be side-tracked with these matters, or she would by now be talking about her servants (those before the Revolution) and of Mr 'M' who was taking care of her horse, Ruby, or of Mr 'D' who had the cow that had calved, which in turn had had calves that had led to (she didn't quite say it) a populated ranch.

Occasionally, when the family watched television together, an old American Western, say, and we saw the stampede of cows, eyes would search one another out briefly, and we would brace ourselves for some mention of the old animal pound which, though not in use from about 1955, was still seen as a secure refuge for our livestock which was clearly threatening to overrun the island: who would go back and round them up? Also, the horse, Ruby, had broken its neck many years before, but we hadn't told her.

The pound, located at the old family home in Coderington, was, like the rest of the house, ruled over by my grandmother till her death in 1954. It was a house, and not the only one, we had sent money back from England, for about fifteen years, to maintain, an empty house, till finances finally forced sense to get the better of pride, and we guiltily asked the house to maintain itself: we allowed no photograph of the consequence to reach my mother's failing eyesight.

So when we met in her room – in Upton Park now, in my married sister's house, though the room seemed much the same as it had done in Maida Vale, in Ladbroke Grove, in Kilburn; cluttered, the television, though newer, still blinking – it was still mid-'50s in St Caesare, in Coderington. It was usually the weekend, relief from Grammar School in neighbouring Montserrat, the family together, the house maintaining its former glory. We brought my grand-mother back to life, setting things again in train, the baking of bread and cakes on the Friday evening, continuing on Saturday with neighbours sometimes using our facilities (two ovens plus a cassava-plate? If they didn't oil the cassava-plate it would rust). And that brought us to Sunday, a busy day with church and entertainment, church all the way to St Anne's, and Sunday School, relieved by the entertainment, perhaps the vicar to lunch or tea if he was preaching in Coderington, perhaps a visit from favoured rela-tives in town. It was good with my grandmother present. If, when we summoned up the house, it was after my grandmother's death, and it was truly empty, our memories tended to falter, disagree-ments emerged, so it was safer always to bring my grandmother back.

I had seen the house, about fifteen years after the Revolution, and the wooden upper portions were sagging. It was proclaimed by neighbours to be dangerous, and I had to confirm, as representative of the family, that this time there would be no long-distance prop of maintenance. After my departure, I'm told, neighbours had started dismantling it, helping themselves not just to doors and windows etc. – and some of the drawing-room windows still had their glass – but to wood which, some say, can be identified in village houses to this day. It was too sentimental a notion but somehow I refused to shoo away the thought; it half-pleased me. Now, a decade and a half later, the house a ruin, my mother destined never to return, the one house (of five) still standing had to claim our attention.

By unspoken consent, in Upton Park when we returned to the family house, we talked of the land, of the flower-garden which I, being the youngest, had tended in the years before I was eleven, of the four grafted mango trees – one for each child: who was the fourth one for? – of the sugarapple and the breadnut and the seagrapes at the front of the house . . .

'At the back of the house. The back.'

'Well . . .'

'The ordinary grapes at the front but the seagrape . . .'

'What does it matter?'

'It does matter. It matters. How can you . . .?'

Yes, the seagrapes were at the back of the house in the sense that they were next to the coal-room downstairs, and that was at the back of the house. But then the coal-room was really at the front of the house; it was under the veranda.

'It wasn't under the veranda.'

'It wasn't *directly* under the veranda. It was at the back of the veranda under mother's room.'

'All right, it was at the back of the veranda.'

'Back of the house.'

Though it was next to the lawn where Nellie spread her sheets, between the coal-room and the water-trough; and that was clearly the front of the house, the entrance to the place, with the fourteen front steps that led up to the veranda.

The seagrapes were in that position, then, on the border of Mrs Meade's land, where I used to sit for hours with John my school-mate from the Meade's house, talking of, among other things, life in familiar places like Canada where it was assumed we'd both end up. (As, indeed, John did, in Toronto.)

'And what's in this cake, it's fantastic!'

'Just plain.'

We're back in the room in Upton Park. Whenever they knew I was coming to visit, my mother would organize the baking of a cake, a special cake without currants and raisins which I had never liked. My grandmother had started the habit years, decades before, of mincing all fruit to be put in the cake, so that it wasn't like fruit any more, no great lumps soiling it, just enriching the texture, uniformly. My sister's version of how this came about is different from mine: she insists that as a somewhat fastidious (or retarded) child, I had confused the currants and raisins with *flies*, and that the mincing operation had been instituted for that reason, to placate me, to indulge me. My version is that it had – and has – everything to do with aesthetics, the sameness of texture as you bite, and little to do with an elementary point about hygiene that could so easily be disproved. But, of course, I'm not prepared to contradict my sister.

I still enjoyed my cake; though there was a mild penalty to be paid. My mother was no longer able to make the cake herself. Her fingers, stiffening, militated against this; so it was left to my nieces, my sister's children, first one then the other – who, brought up a stone's throw from supermarkets, couldn't appreciate the logic of *making* cakes oneself – to make my fruitless cake. For by now it *had* become fruitless, the mincing fad being dropped. I praised my nieces for having made the cake the traditional way, first beating the dozen eggs with the fork, then the melted butter, then the sugar etc., all of course done manually, as in the old house in Coderington; and they indulged me.

'Fabulous cake. What's in it?'

'That thing you like,' that was my mother. 'What you call it again?'

'What, you put *money* in it?' Only my mother found this amusing; there were about five of us present. So I tried again, savouring the cake:

'Nutmeg. No, not nutmeg.' (I thought of a joke about nutmeg, but on reflection, decided to save it.) 'Not nutmeg, is it?'

'No, no, no. That other thing you like.' The others weren't playing; though they appreciated the mild entertainment. Finally, my niece prevented it becoming tedious.

'It's cinnamon.' I connected this and various spices and herbs with other parts of my life, with Indian and Chinese and Middle-Eastern homes in which I'd eaten, with various continental doings, with things vaguely foreign, but not particularly with this house.

'We used to have that at home,' my mother remembered.

'Cinnamon!' No one else could remember that.

'Yes, yes.'

'What, in Coderington?'

'Of course, in the garden. In the grounds. We had it.'

Eyes met each other surreptitiously to indicate that everyone was thinking along the same lines: more goodies we had left behind; every year, it seemed, our abandoned wealth grew greater.

'We used to put it in the cake all the time,' my mother continued.

'*My* mother. Mammie.'

My sister indicated that I shouldn't pursue it. I had a tendency, which irritated others, of pursuing these things too far, the idea being that accuracy of recall was more healthy in the end than a complete slide into fantasy. But.

'It used to grow behind the house.'

And that was the last time I had my mother's cake.

And here I am at the house in Coderington, the ruin. 'The absence of ruins.' They should know of this family. The funeral is tomorrow; her request not to be buried in England, honoured. I've had to hack my way through to the foundations, bush reclaiming our home – inheritors of the Revolution building their villas elsewhere, on the more fashionable side of the island. Coconuts litter the ground, sprouting; guava trees everywhere: I had the idea of a guava-jelly industry. I've got a man helping me to identify the bushes, the trees – where are the grafted mangoes? – in this place where I lived till I was eleven, which was still home till I was sixteen. But the dream last night was unsettling enough to drive me here.

I'd just flown out from England, tired, fluey, staying in Montserrat with family. I dreamt that I was back at the house leaving *for* London. The same age as in 1956, but with a difference. Instead of the long-packed over-readiness of that time, waiting for the months to pass as you labelled and re-labelled suitcases, now there was a mass scramble, my brother and I – my sister was absent from the dream – heading for England. We had already lived in England for decades and we were heading early in the morning for Marble Arch, which was, of course, at the bottom of the hill, through the fields. Someone – my brother's wife – suggested breakfast before we set out. At that point my brother becomes my sister, and we discover together that we have more space in our luggage than we thought. Books. My own book, already written in my grandmother's time, is inserted. Several copies. The bread-room bustling. Early-morning breakfast smells. People. I'm watching the time. I set out, without my luggage, through the fields, for something or other. A man connected with the house comes to assist. He has a car. I get into the car. As we start descending I decide to go to Marble Arch and check in. Marble Arch can't be more than fifteen minutes away.

Problems. We get lost; ask directions; get sent on. It looks, in retrospect, neither like Marble Arch nor like Coderington. Though I only half-think so then. We go, film-like, on foot, through buildings. One is a hotel. I open the door; the side of the building comes away – a cardboard suitcase. There's a man inside asleep, in bed: I close the door, the wall, gently, so as not to wake him, and escape through another room – not the hotel but a house joined to it, down-market. Here, there's a middle-aged man (the people are white) putting on his trousers. I tip-toe past him towards the open window. Ground floor. Without turning, he's ready for this, accustomed to it, bangs on the wall of the hotel for assistance. The hotel doesn't fall. Maybe I didn't think, till later, that it might fall. I escape, take directions. I am pursued and suddenly made conscious that my dress is distinctive. Though the dream gets it wrong for these distinctive clothes are already in my suitcase and I am dressed soberly. An hour later, I haven't got to Marble Arch. I miss my plane, my brother nowhere in sight, the bulk of my luggage still at the house . . .

At the house, hacking through the grass, I wasn't looking for luggage. My guide is still pointing out the guavas: to him I'm a stranger, almost a tourist. The *wanga* trees I remember, though not the name; the *calabash*, of course, so close to the house: I'm pleased with this, a little bit of Africa in our yard. No calabashes on it, though. The *stinking cedar tree* was one of the circle that defined the animal pound. Maybe there are others. Impossible to see. Too much foliage. But cool here. A good place to build, to grow up, away from the heat of Barville. I passed quickly over the *burial ground grass* – good for tea, he said, bush tea – it was different from the *long grass*, the *long grass* was rubbish: he picked some and put it in his bag (he was from the town). So much fern everywhere. That put me in mind of harvest. Harvest Sunday. I was grateful to focus on the *soursop* trees, behind the water-trough, flourishing: who had eaten the soursop for thirty-three years? Could I approach a man at random and demand reparation for thirty-three years of soursop? It would work in a play: did he deserve to go scot-free with my mother dead? I had to suppress other thoughts. She had looked girlish in the coffin, teeth protruding a little – like that Pope, a while back, John Paul – and this upset some of the family. She was a beautiful woman to the end. And the world never let her believe it; and we hadn't restructured the world – no aesthetic *perestroika* in the family: we had accommodated the world, she doubted she was beautiful . . . I was beginning not to like my mood.

Ah, the mango trees! . . . Grafted mangoes? No, no grafted mangoes here.

'Where're the grafted mangoes?'

'They not grafted mangoes. No grafted mangoes here.'

(No grafted mangoes? A page torn out of your youth. Lucky you're not a book.)

Not grafted but hairy mango; pap mango.

'Pop?'

'Pap?'

'Yes, the small ones. Small and sour.'

'Not so sour. Sometimes, they sweet.'

And a quick, less patient run-through now, of the *chuckle-rock* that boys used to play marbles with. I remembered the *chuckle-rock* though not the name, and I didn't remember, particularly, playing marbles with them, I remember playing marbles with marbles: we used to get bundles of them, from Canada or somewhere, and my mother used to dole them out, maybe half-a-dozen or so at a time, and when you lost them, or had them won from you – because we were never among the champion marble-players – she would dole out another half-dozen.

Then a startling thing which sent prickles through my body. We were inside the foundations, we had to hack our way through, break branches (I suffered the mild but recurring fear of a snake, as you couldn't always see where you were putting your foot; and the occasional ground-lizard scurrying away made you melt). So we were standing in what would have been the kitchen, though the wall that separated it from the bread-room to the right had gone: maybe it was wooden, though I didn't think it was, facing the big room at the back of the house, which had been added in my time. It was never used except for storing lumber and things like that; and my old pet goat which would be brought in there at nights, my grandmother's favour to me, to prevent it having to be put in the pound, which was a public sort of place; that was for animals to be auctioned after their six-week stay, and for our own pigs; but then pigs were pigs. On top of this spare room at the back of the house was the upstairs bathroom and loo, the water-closet. Showering there was a test of nerve, for behind the overhead pipes, you were always likely to find a wood-slave, the most disgusting sort of lizard, trying to keep itself cool. These creatures had the habit of falling off the pipes, but doing it very slowly, parts of them hanging in the air for minutes. It was often too messy to drive them out, too unnerving to kill them, so you took your chances underneath, flesh creeping at the thought of what might fall on you.

Well, this 'upper room' was not open to the sky as expected, but overhung by a giant tree and leaves giving it the appearance of being protected; and sitting in the solid concrete bath – not a crack on it – secure still on its concrete frame, clamped to the outside wall, concrete looking so new, – sitting there, tomb-like, was a growth. The luxurious clump seemed too well-positioned, too settled, too arrogant in its placing for it to be an accident. The man, the guide, told me the name of the bush and I didn't register it; I distracted myself. I thought of – I don't know what I thought of. I thought of ... Cleopatra in her barge. I thought of ... the ship on which we came to England ... I thought of giant containers pregnant with fruit. There was something womanly about the bush – the *cheney bush*. Or was it *hard-leaf*? – the broad leaves which traditionally had been used to wrap the *duckna*; they also fed the leaves to pigs, and rope-like roots hanging straight down, metres-long, used also to tie up the *duckna*, used as string.

I had to go outside. I heard the commentary but took little note of what corresponded to the *bread and cheese* tree or the *turkey-berry* or the *money-bush* (though this last, on the borders of the dining and servant rooms, I remembered as the one with little leaves that closed up when you touched them, and my guide said they made good tea, when you were restless or had bad dreams). I was standing outside now at the back of the house, next to the little copper cistern that had been a huge *bassin* when we were young. The *loploy* outside the coal-room window didn't divert me as I stood facing the huge grape trees – not vines – reddish-brown, massive; they couldn't possibly bear grapes now: I was thinking, are they at the front of the house or the back of the house? when my guide, his back to me, continued:

'And over there you got the cinnamon bush.'

'The what?' He wasn't a practical joker, so I turned, stumbled through the foliage, got caught up in roots, got pricked, felt childhood things falling lightly on my neck and finally, without guilt, crushed a leaf from the bush – a small tree – and smelt it: *cinnamon*.

The next day we buried my mother, and with her, I expect, many secrets from the Life Before the Revolution.

Reunion

I'm in these ridiculous clothes, a tie, jacket. Fortunately, the heat might permit me to carry the jacket over my arm, wear the waistcoat instead; the waistcoat is lighter-coloured: a compromise. I'm driving ... south, I suppose, instead of east, away from the scene of the – can't settle on the word for it – burial in the family plot isn't the sum of it. I'm a stranger here now, a visitor who comes from time to time, having to acknowledge people on the road, every outing a sort of PR exercise; you have to look good, be polite, gracious. (*I have lived abroad, I have acquired the responsibility of graciousness.*) Have to look good, justify all those years abroad; people seem to forgive you almost anything if you're perceived to have done well abroad: is that why she never came back, except to be buried? Don't ... remember to wave to anyone who looks as if he, she might know you, then you won't have people say things have gone to your head (even though they might excuse it on this occasion). ... And here I am in these ridiculous clothes. Not as sticky as I feared, good time of year, a breeze; April. Remember to come back again in April; might even wear the coat over the waistcoat, light-coloured waistcoat, sports coat, dark, subtly different shade from the trousers. That'll do. Must go back and pick up Paul and Anna at the hotel. (Why must I invent Paul and Anna as travelling companions? Aren't the family enough?) Still time to get back to the family.

'You don't have the time,' my mother's voice. As always I would pretend to misunderstand, seek to show how the five or six tasks I'd set myself on that particular visit could be accomplished before going-home time. She would explain a little impatiently that that was not what she meant, she was talking about the old habit of not giving a clue to family and friends of how to measure whether I was heading for destitution or respectability; meanwhile, grey hairs on a child, still a child, was bound to make a parent anxious.

'Oh, I've got plenty of time,' I would insist: *here am I in '56, learning to make ladies' belts; this one shows me an expert at making ladies' belts. Three years. Then a bit of reading – all those books. Three years. Six years in a lifetime. OK, there was the odd play that failed, but ... Time, yet, to match the success of that boy [supply name] I went to school with, the boy who ended up in Canada. Time to rebuild the old family house in St Caesare. Ah, but I'm ready for that; here are the pictures of the building.* That should wipe the memory of failed plays or the failed ladies'-belt project: the couple of dozen skins of leather – leather and suède – never getting to the point of restraining the waist of strange women, of press-studding them into 22, 24, 26" portions of flesh; the challenge of it. Surely, against *some* law of the imagination! Ah, but rivals pushed on, got there, made the belts. (In contrition, in revenge, I wrote you into the belt-factory scene in the play; you exercised your rights as a character not to be abused, and the play failed.) Easier to use Philosophy – *Philosophy & English* – to measure yourself against this or that school-friend.

And we're back in London, in her room upstairs, in Upton Park. (If I had imagination I'd give you a new country (would you like Poland?) to be Linda the Great of. *And a new play: Always hold a wine glass in your up-stage hand!*) She's peering at the photograph of the unfinished house.

'It finished? It's not finished.'

It was open to the sky. 'No, only two-thirds finished.'

'It's your house?'

'Yes, I have a partner.'

'It's not yours.'

'Well, I have a partner.'

'It look funny. Looks funny.'

'Well it's . . . it is a bit.'

'I don't recognize it. It's not like my house at all. Our house.'

'It's in France. They build them differently there.'

'You shouldn't build it in France, you should build it at home. The foundations still standing.'

'Next time. Next time, we're going to do that.'

'This is a small house, how many rooms you have?'

'We're not thinking in terms of . . .'

'You don't have twelve rooms. Our house had twelve rooms, you remember?'

'Well, you know. Well, anyway, we've got three bedrooms.'

'Three?'

'Double bedrooms. And three bathrooms.'

That last was a source of mild amusement. 'Three bathrooms?'

Laying it on now. 'And the pool. Swimming pool.'

A pause for thought. 'I don't think I like the idea of those things.'

'Swimming pools?'

'Oh no ... with other people using it. Not clean. Just not clean. You have to be careful.'

'We'll clean it once a year,' wickedly.

'Ohhh,' a shudder of distaste.

'And then when you come down, we'll teach you to swim.' But she had by then begun to tire of the game.

'You should build it at home,' she said simply.

And here I am now driving, in these ridiculous clothes. Must pick up Anna and Paul. Paul won't play the guitar, but another instrument, the flute, or a mouth-organ, something classless, and recite from the pulpit something heavy and *young* about Peace on Earth and protecting the environment, yes, for the beast of the field, the fowl and the fish, preferably in rhyming couplets – before ending with a hymn from the Methodist Hymnal, the more archaic the better, one full of *thous* and *thees* and inversions. And then Anna would follow and do her solo, without music, Dietrich-voiced, like at the inauguration of a President; and it would be good if it were in a foreign language, German and sentimental, or French, Piaf-like. I created them, those two, they would do that for me. I created them in France a few months ago, that night I drove the Renault off the road. Ideal mourners. (Ridiculous thought: what if I didn't, in fact, walk out of it, that night in Feyance, and am dead! No, I wouldn't be driving as badly now, some things change, surely, in the after-life. Too stupid to pinch yourself.)

As a compromise I raise my arm, languidly, wave at someone who hesitates and reacts as if she's not the sort of person I (someone in this car) might be expected to know; she raises her hand. That's it, then; I'm here to attend another's funeral, someone old and threatening as a mother. *She couldn't have wanted that!* But I pull up sharply, slightly surprising myself, and start turning round; there are people to pick up, then we must head east.

But the night in France, in Feyance, is back with a vengeance. As I burst through the chain of the petrol-station, waking up before I crash, I think, absurdly, of being in an unmarked grave, and for some reason, invent the comic duo, Paul and Anna, as witness; they'll do the honours. With Paul, Dali-like, swimming trunks, complete with dog on lead, and Anna in heels and dark stockings, suspendered, I would hide behind that. And it works: the head clears (I think now of those not-quite-hour-glass things, filled with water and sand: you turn it over, it's cloudy for a bit and then it clears). So there I am wedged in the car from the impact; I check, surreptitiously, the seat-belt; and wait. The last I remember before dropping off was the World Service News. Midnight. Midnight-thirty, as they say. But now it's pop music: same station? Or has the impact shifted it? – *something to dine out on*. I'm not hurt, there's no panic. Paul and Anna can sink back into oblivion.

We had been working on the house – the house that was in the wrong place, wrong country, not the family home – at Montauroux, day after day, more than seven days a week, plunging into debt, bad weather, bad moods, falling behind schedule – the first let slipping away, the first tenant fantasizing two weeks among the olives, pine and oak, yet to be disappointed. Though the house was 'finished', we were there or thereabouts, as cricket commentators say when the ball was *just* missing the wicket. We had completed the furnishing that day, that evening – two late trips in a hired van down the autoroute to Mandelieu, the hypermarket near Cannes. Following in the car, I'd drifted off behind the wheel for a few seconds, and hoped that had scared me into sense. So, leaving the 'furnished' house, past midnight, back to friends in Seillans where I'd been sleeping, twenty minutes away, I permitted myself to relax. They'd be in bed, of course; I'd be too tired to shower, probably, or to eat; but the change of scene preserved your sanity. That's when it happened: I woke as the chain to the petrol station snapped across the bonnet of the Renault and the car wedged itself in the cast-iron frame of the café awning next door. Middle of Feyance; the cross-roads. Nothing, for who knows how long. The commotion, the advance party of an enemy rising in the night, armed – I could pick out the odd garden tool or farming implement; one man was wearing a night-shirt: my fleeting image, something coming at me out of Chaucer. Ah, but that's really another story.

Sweating slightly in my funeral clothes, I return not to the hotel but to a cousin's place to find I have missed the rest of the family. My explanations are accepted before I make them. There are others waiting for a lift; I'm redirected to service them. They too have come a long way for this; from overseas, couldn't make them late: *don't lose your way and pretend to be foreign. Don't pull rank because of the occasion; don't crash and be pathetic; be the host, be coherent, thank them for coming . . .*

Well, we have to get back to it sometime; the signing of the Visitors' Book in the nave of the church next to the coffin, *the coffin*; beautiful wood, beautiful *sheen*, with its transparent window – she looked so young and small, the gown with a suggestion of a frill at the neck, girlish in a sort of . . . German way: how could she have died, *lived* without ever having uttered a word of German – *a new scene for the play, a new sequence for the novel – replacing the belt-factory effort?* But for now there's the blundering through hand-shakes, pretending to remember people, some so old and polished and church-dressed (*are they waiting to be put into a book, to be painted?*), dressed for church thirty years ago, the suits, the dresses fitting bodies not yet this shape.

Relief, though, at the organ, the choir. The choir strangely beautiful: why had I denied myself this experience over the years? I settled down in the front pew with the family, a foot from the coffin in its new position; and here the tricks started. Hymn No. 50 – 'The Lord's My Shepherd' – attacked the hand, though the prayers, following, offered some relief. But the next hymn, No. 526 – 'O Jesus, I Have Promised' – again starts the hand shaking, attacks the eyes, the knees; I had to sit down. Another member of the family also sitting while all else stand and sing: they are strong. I look up and see Paul standing at the lectern (*What is this? Concentrate, concentrate*), not the big lectern on the upper pulpit, one of the two on the lower platform, the left one facing me, opposite. (*I fancy all eyes are on me for this.*) What's he saying, he doesn't have his guitar, he's saying something, it's in rhyme; he's got the audience with him, the congregation; this is almost developing into a call and response thing. Everyone seems to know the words, even those not responding out loud, using body-language; you could sense the rightness of it. That feels better, makes it easier to wipe the glasses. The man up there is talking of faith in expansive, semi-coloned phrases, a new style, *a very old style*; how elegant, how easy to listen to: *is this right?* It's my brother, of course, reading from *Hebrews*.

So that's the way out! I, too, will read from The Book, find a passage about building in the wrong place. The next hymn is soothing, everything's in working order, I can hear my own voice. (I can hear Anna's too, but won't look in her direction.) With hymn

No. 527 – 'Sometimes a Light Surprises' – we're back, secure, with the family; a favourite hymn going back generations. And so to *Revelations* 7:9–17, read by a brother, and the Eulogy. (The eulogy, delivered by an old school-friend, not seen in thirty years, living on another continent, is about generosity; is generous, *is all that's missing from my play, my novel: I won't make her speak German, I won't give her a strange name, I need more time.*) 'Oh Jesus, I Have Promised' (No. 526) brings me back to why we're here.

Unseen, the accordion player, *Tie a Yellow Ribbon Round Her Hair* etc. walks us through the field to the graveyard. Everything looks as if it's been there a long time; the green, the broken headstones, except the raw, brown 'family' soil. Even the black and white costume drama: cool, soft dresses, elegant hats, white against black, black against black: *has anyone written of this beauty?* Little knots among the tomb-stones, composed, singing, chatting, reassuring; singing voices, young and resonant, belying the faces.

I choose to forget the rest, but remember the pleasing coolness of April, and in the car home someone saying that *she* was universally loved, that she was generous; and I can hear her (for mine ears only) objecting to being spoken of as if she wasn't present. I reassure her; of course, she answers in a foreign language, maybe German: this exchange lasts the entire scene. And in the back of the car someone is saying that God is good.

The Gift

I had inherited two books from my mother; I considered, instead, the Bible and the walking stick; then I returned to the two books.

Just think of the wild people in our family, *yeah, yegggghhh*. Ah, well. But some families revel in practical jokes. You see them on television: they spend so much energy thinking up surprises, surprises which might cause embarrassment, temporarily, but which in the end enable them to fall into one another's arms, with relief and laughter, with a few tears perhaps; a unit affirmed, strengthened by the experience. How do we compare with this?

I suppose the closest we came to it was with an uncle who lived abroad for much of his life and became a priest, and there was always a question mark about his credentials, his degrees, over where he went to university, to theological college; but he sported a DD in the end – Doctor of Divinity – so much more imposing than mere doctors of Music or Dentistry – though not quite up there with an MD, particularly one who specialized in an area we couldn't spell. He made sure the whole island knew of his elevation, by writing letters to all sorts of people on one pretext or another – even to us; and his headed notepaper said it all: The Very Reverend A. S. Stapleton DD, with a couple of minor degrees thrown in. What was interesting, though, was that the fellow never lost his nerve. Before he died, he bequeathed his DD to a young cousin. He left it in his will as you might leave a house or a bit of land, as you might leave a valued possession, secure in the family. And this boy, this, cousin, accepting the gift in the spirit in which it was given, decided there and then to put it to use, and was now preaching sermons successfully, in Canada, a Very Reverend DD.

But we tend to disown such rogues in the family. They are accused of indulging in non-familial behaviour, convicted *in absentia*, and banished to the Americas. That leaves us secure in our universe, dull and dependable. Of course, some of us, secretly, wanted to upstage the rogues. *We had talked, mother to son, sort of thing, whispered it, of ways of being up there with the wild people. I wasn't allowed to run and jump and be hit in the face (unworthy, tacky) or even to be good at cricket (best kept as a benchmark) so I would reclaim territory lost to the family on this or that continent in other ways.)*

67

I'd vowed to restore the majesty of our entrances and exits: how to leave this country, how to enter this house, that had been botched. In an early house in Ladbroke Grove, we had moved in while workmen were still pottering; and you could detect that the plumber, a slow, heavy man whose clothes were trained to take his shape, was not enamoured at our being there while he worked on the geyser. (My mother, middle-aged, was holding a baby: was the baby, the plumber asked, quietly alarmed, her own? Oh no, *condescendingly*. And in walked the daughter – in strode the daughter, leggy, sequined, eyelashes and lips flashing: *Now he's leaning on mah shoul-der. Mammah, he's kissin' me-eee*, the choir-trained voice, made for TV – (you've got TV?) – in walked the daughter of child-bearing age, mother of the child: relief all round.) In the end the plumber was won over, accepted a cup of tea, fought down the panic that it was good, and sought to pay for it in his way: 'You're Christian people, aren't you? Gentle people,' he said . . .

Mother, indignant that anyone should doubt that we were Christian people, the rest of us bristling at being called 'gentle', the baby storing her comment for later . . . is this what we'd come to, our resources stretched to accommodate a doubting plumber! I vowed to restage this entry to our house, or at least deny him the prestige of installing our new Italian fridge, a Zanussi. (When, three years later, Mosley staged a rally outside that house, I rewrote the play.)

And here was I, thirty-odd wasted years later, gift in hand, biting back accusation, pulling against regret insubstantial as cloud. I had collected two books from her room, with my name on. *I'll shift all this to Florence, the death-bed scene; she's too weak to accompany us to the Uffizi, which has just honoured her grand-daughter, artist in the family*. But this dissolves into an earlier farce, the 'German' period, I call it: *Eigenleben*, I say aloud, bringing it back. I seem to remember the Germans used the word in art criticism to indicate that the author no longer has control over his, over her creation, can no longer be possessive of it once it's been made public (is that why I hang back?). So my mother, dying, leaving me two books that I had written and given to her, is not returning my gift, but passing on something of her own. I accept the gift. *Eigenleben*.

I scanned the room; someone had been here before me and tampered with the evidence, the 'da Firenze' had gone, the work of a niece, obviously. There were, in one phase of the family, three painters who mattered: Leonardo and Michelangelo, neither of whom *really* mattered, and da Firenze, who did. (The Italian connection was a sort of running near-joke going back beyond the accident of having come to England on an Italian boat in 1956. Before the journey someone had the idea of marking the send-off by having a painter, a local boy who'd been abroad and come back with an Italian name, paint scenes from the house to keep it intact – the animal pound, my mother on the horse; us on the veranda, that sort of thing: he had called himself da Firenze. Much later, in England, when my schoolgirl nieces showed small aptitude for drawing or painting, the results were promptly dubbed 'da Firenzes'. One niece finally managed to overcome this handicap by moving smartly into politics, impressing us with her study of American Presidents, commenting on their physiognomy – did you know that Eisenhower was the first smiling President (in his official photograph)? After that they all smiled, with the exception of LBJ, who had his mouth open but managed not to smile. Before that no one smiled, unless you call the expression on the face of Herbert Clarke Hoover a smile, and it wasn't a smile. The two she singled out at the opposite end of the scale – and that's going way back to nos. 4 and 7 – were John Quincy Adams and Andrew Jackson. Hammer-horror types. Especially Jackson. Adams was more the mad scientist, all whiskers and, you know, family secrets, the superior butler. As she developed her theory into a political ideology she found it necessary to repudiate da Firenze, going through the house confiscating and destroying them. She had preceded me here in this room: I couldn't destroy these books, I had no American Presidents to put in their place.

The books I had given my mother could have afforded little enjoyment; they were 'difficult'; poetry. They could not even be presented as a badge of worldly success; mine wasn't a position similar to Vonnegut's, say, who, when he presented his best-sellers to the family was reputedly told: 'We don't understand your books, but we're glad you're rich.' That option wasn't open to us with these books: if you can't see them as commerce, you've got somehow to try and pass them off as art; and my mother did make an attempt. On receiving the first book, she had opened it at random and commented on a poem: why were the stanzas of unequal length? Oddly enough, I was unprepared for this. When I wrote the poems I hadn't been thinking of formal tidiness, not in terms of quatrains and the like, in ways to which my mother would have become accustomed from the hymns of Charles Wesley and other *savants* of the Methodist Hymnal. That had an effect on confidence; these jagged lines, these lumps of what might no longer be energy, represented not people we knew, but malformed creatures, incomplete. I had seen a TV programme about people in contemporary Russia reciting Pushkin. The camera had roamed round certain Leningrad streets on a weekend when bakers and housewives and policemen dressed themselves up as Pushkin characters – ladies in carriages, the lot – reciting bits of Pushkin's poems: a city-wide people's theatre. I thought, then, looking at the book in my mother's hand, that if my lines were to be intoned by persons whose portraits I had drawn, they would be *sullen* with regret, they would be *joyless*; worse, they would lisp and splutter and forget and *lie*; they would, in effect, dishonour the family. My mother never asked about aesthetic matters again; although a later comment, in response to the second book – 'When are you going to write a book that we can understand?' – came close.

I hadn't promised a book she would understand, that would be to tempt fate. *Here I am reworking a scene from the old house, grandmother as matriarch; a big scene recalling an auction from the animal pound. There she is at the top of the steps, the back steps, sitting on the floor of her room, fourteen steps up, the village gathered, butcher, neighbours etc. to bid for the pig. Nellie and Sarah from the house, to make up the numbers. I bid on behalf of the house. This scene may or may not be retained in my adaptation of* The Cherry Orchard, *set here.*) Ah, hard to imagine a life after life. One must grow up, perhaps, grow out of false starts.

I'm dreaming, she says to me, not my mother but a young woman of my acquaintance; she says: 'Now I must get you into China!' This is an old joke. As a child, I remember, my grandmother had promised me China. I was, of course, a heathen and, with my cousin Horace and a couple of other boys, had formed a society of *heathens*, primed to desecrate the islands' churches, though my grandmother couldn't have known that. (She may have talked, directly, to God.) She had heard that in China all people were heathens, and China being a country of many people, and God being merciful, something would have to be done not to damn the many heathens in China. Sadly, since I could not be saved, the safest thing was to hide me among the Chinese who, by sheer weight of numbers, might appeal to the God of mercy rather than the God of vengeance. (*Vengeance is mine, saith the Lord.*) When someone said the Chinese were blackish rather than whitish, that clinched it. And I had duly gone to China.

This was later. I had found myself in Australia, in Sydney, and went to the doctor's – a friend's doctor in Balmain – to be inoculated against hepatitis for my trip to China; and the man was gracious, urbane (Urbane of Balmain?), had been, himself, to China, and urged me to visit the Peace Hotel in Shanghai to enjoy the jazz. He was intrigued that I was a poet, and declined payment. Naturally, I offered him a copy of the book I toured with – my calling card – and avoided getting hepatitis in China: a good transaction, the book cost £5.95. On several occasions since, the book has been a cross between passport and currency – gaining me dinner, services, travel and the simple exchange of gifts. My friends, wickedly, cost my world at £5.95. I say to this or that distant General or local bully: do not invade, do not violate. I am backed by £5.95 worth of moral authority; it derives from the old house, it is backed up by a niece's da Firenze. We're not just recouping family losses, I say; we've come to reinforce those without armies and tanks ... at these moments of danger to self, my friend, a woman of my acquaintance, says to me, 'Now, I must get you into China.'

I juggle Bible, walking-stick and two books. No one in the family has thought of growing three hands. See, now I'm priest, witch-doctor; magic. Fear me, hear my sermon: *It was bad, O Lord, to have come from a small island to a small island; the mind lay undisturbed in its village, unstretched.* I would have carried this off had the DD devolved to me. But my congregation knows this to be a lie; I have travelled too much, perhaps, too far – first to a nation in contraction, *not good thing* the intellect pulling one way, the ego another; your life becomes an essay in 'Excuse'.

In the new book our heroine – call her La Contessa – learns to drive a car, to swim, goes to the beach, finds it threatening. We're accompanied by friends from daytime TV. I protect the beach. I'm armed with my niece's thesis on the physiognomy of Presidents. I speak out of the side of my mouth: 'You're a dead man,' I say, to someone who challenges the story of the house. Though I might just quote from a good book. Or tell about my time in China.

71

VI

Cricket

Again, Andrew

i.m. Andrew Salkey, 1928–1995

The 'idiot' will score runs, will take wickets and save us.
(Yes, it would be nice if the boys were to play their bauxite
instead of bat and ball, but we love that, too, despite protests.)
Your gap prods me to explain the jokes, like pulling faces
at those big, slow-moving boys who will bear our name
(then one of them, at Amherst, loped through our conversation,
shaming us with politeness, allowing pride to surface. The talk,
    now,
was of little miners and their healthy sons in plays of the '50s).

Ah, this is disingenuous, to disguise what we felt, that *this*
was our best place, our only place, that there is no better place;
and we leave it when we must, without result –
to that man with views we campaigned against, healthy with his
    family;
to the 'idiots' moving up the order. And, with luck, to a partner
    among the quick,
to slow-moving boys growing into family – our team holding its
    shape.

Not Cricket

He's part of the attack; think of dark
alleys, crowd-applause.
And presenting this match as one against one
when geed by his pals, all ten of them,
with the victim no longer whistling for courage,
sort of thing . . . this is the charge.
We won't hear her self-blaming song, handed down,
women saying 'ouch' from the crease: this is the charge.

So he retched at killings and maimings
on the news, *comes* over her, then in dream
betrays all to the team
elevating group pressure to an art. And, yes,
she's allowed to defend herself within the rules:
her batting on display, our 'feel-good' factor.

Long Shot

Funny the film won awards even at Cannes,
for it lacked something. So the boys at home
supplied the commentary, filling in detail, freezing
each shot in pretend close-up, talking our heroes
up to size. For we don't look good
in a world obsessed with war and famine
threatening to change the name of the game
which guarantees our place in the sun.

The Test Match scene in long shot was an insult.
The acrobatic catch in the slips; our man
making impossible saves on the boundary . . .
And then batting and bowling that wins
countries their independence: we're not ants, smudges
of black'n'white in a world too large to care who wins, loses.

Conversations at Upton Park *iii*

She's padded up, ready to come in at No. 3 for West Indies.
But the gloves are a problem for fingers
All tender and arthritic. And she'll need a runner.
But other pioneers in the family faced worse
Than short-pitched bowling and sledging. Her eldest son,
You know, cleared mines in Africa: that's how he lost his leg.
So, really, it's not asking much of the rest
To make an effort and pull West Indies through.

She is confused whether we're strong or weak,
A question unanswered since uncle George came back from Panama
Without his speech. *Strong* you went for a win, *weak* you tried
To avoid defeat: was that a way to live? We're not mean-
Spirited, we don't boycott football because the rightful heir
Can't kick. Now she needs someone to follow her instructions – like
    that boy Lara.

For Brian Lara

'But he lifting up the bat too high! . . .
You can't afford to lift up the bat so high.'
'But you got to lift up the bat so high,' we say, stirring it.
Though Mammie, in TV glasses, knows what she knows
and backs her bet with a look.
And, in truth, with the quickies sulking on the boundary
some slow foolishness nearly sneak through, even though
the boy, headstrong as ever, reach his century lifting up the bat.

Is sad, but not a tragedy when your luck run out,
for no man, however brilliant, can live forever
at the crease. And as one commentator was heard to say –
not Mammie, she speak for herself – Fellow said: you have to
    careful
of some little forceripe spinner who just come on and push up he
    han',
push up he han', and then bowl you a straight ball.

VII

From a Secret History

Family Reunion

She knows this is the, ah, Piccadilly
Line and claims credit. 'Fat Legs' shows off odd
socks her sister, still reading, dubs silly,
to show how to survive two weeks with dad.
Both girls agree it was a close-run thing,
him speaking *Welsh* at supper more than once
and singing in a high-pitched voice to bring
on nightmares. And this could be the last chance

with mum returning from America,
to use dad, who bit her arm, as *pillow*,
fists and head cancelling pre-America
promise not to fight someone all *pillow*
with glasses. Easy. Now for one last show
of strength on this slow train home from Heathrow.

The Elder Sister

Dad said I shouldn't trap Pinkie all the time
into contradicting herself as that's
unkind. But what's the point in being nine
next month, and best at logic winning lots
of quizzes, except to lord it over
someone still silly. For who knows whether
she won't grow up a terrorist with her
gun forcing us all to call her clever?

And, yes, the mum's tight smile and nod disarm
passengers on the train who size up dad,
proud-sheepish now, his tabloid squirm NO HARM
DONE I'M ON THE SIDE OF GOOD so obvious.
He signals truce and she thinks not too bad
having prepared herself for something worse.

From a Line Remembered or Imagined

A daughter's cleverness outdoes your fears,
and you know two adults calming her is the stuff
of nightmare: she's less than a decade old
and can't digest the new fact that everything she knows
her parents know. (Years ago a neighbour's Rolls Royce boy
was delivered back to the island, connections in his head
flooded. But we're elsewhere.) This is not something
a girl can live with. You reel on a decade

to see her matching skill to threat, paramedics
taking liberties. Time to count sheep: these things she knows
that you don't know – the name of a character on daytime
        television;
what one boy said at school about his *inkling*; how she fled
the shop that day, with her friend, without paying –
and in sleep, she's your first car, disappearing down the road.

Doctor Philpot

So what's to be said about Philpot? – a promise,
a plague that visited us early and stains
the blood: prison visits have fallen off.
In the days of wish-fulfilment when the boys loped around
Ladbroke Grove and Manor House auditioning for whores
and novelists, Philpot was no more Philpot
than an actor in LT uniform vowing to crash his rush-hour
bus with all hands: *menace, boy, menace*.

Philpot, as if running for office, has supporters
on the loose: though he threatened to chop off
this gesture, to cut out that prejudice, and vigilanted a creature
who made your women take the long way home,
he practised surgery on no one, despite the rash
of provocation: not a doctor, then, more a myth of patience.

Haynestime

Good he should come into his own
after years of exile, fighting, they say,
on foreign soil. As befits a man
of mystery Haynes refuses to confirm
the title won in campaigns
not written up. And here he is
in a downstairs flat, protection
for the family camped above.

Some say it will take a generation
to restore Haynes to family. Pioneers from this house
send progress reports like illnesses hard to spell:
there's been a Doctor, a something else; now
a Commander. The family talk of turning him in.
But out of the window it's growing dark; they sleep on it.

Kreuger

You might say I'm the Lit. Crit. of thieves.
Quote me . . . this is a found villa in the Alpes
Maritimes when the village was out to lunch.
It's all here to be picked over
if you're a student of rubble. As demolisher
I footnote France, Italy, Mediterranean
Turkey to those turned on by ruins,
and supply the tourist guides at a price. Nice.

So Kreuger & Kreuger – business flourishing, money
laundered – is looking good. Time soon to retire
and amuse the children's children with tales of local
colour: *and then we moved into that Sylvan
time, the little town abandoned, its people at sacrifice –*
and realized there was nobody minding the shop. Ah, the old days!

The Origins of Kreuger

Forget about pre-Columbian hurricanes
and volcanoes, or some Mitteleuropa
crucible with sparks arching the centuries
to us. Kreuger, wilful and proud, is family
with a change of name to protect the innocent.
Though his mother thinks him truthful and others
at fault. The family, village-wide, has put money
on this winner to return a doctor with a difference.

The AK-47 has been named and tested.
Land, women and chattel of the enemy long coveted.
Very Reverends are ten-a-penny, and poets
need no foreign training. The boy, dismayed,
turns the clock back, speeds the clock up:
competing screams and whisperings alarm the mother.

Aftermath

Is the third day of the hurricane that last ten hours,
work that out, pardner, that's St Caesare logic for you.
Phase one; and the big boys assemble – the Castine reinstated
in his robes, priestly and fat; the Governor, of course,
and Haynes, the Commander with, they call them epaulettes won
     abroad –
to digest the lessons of this thing.
So what ritual from the ancients go satisfy
this rampant god of wind and biblical foolishness?

Confessions, confessions: that we're all t'iefing & lyin'
and covet our neighbour is old hat and won't impress this
     Equalizer;
so the men must line up to take a beating for the cause.
Phase two: Golly Miss Molly and her likely women, the new militia,
will rain down licks to show the brutes what it's like. That storm
bathed us for two days and nights, and now like the whole island
     satisfy.

Reunion

Now we're fallen from grace and interest
(for we never held office, the old gang
from Ladbroke Grove days) we meet
once a year, or maybe twice a decade to put the past
into some kind of perspective. As always
what's hidden on the agenda is power – who didn't crash
his rush-hour bus, though provoked, didn't poison patients
at the hotel, guests in the hospital, didn't fail *those* students . . .

File these Minutes under 'The Resistance'.
Pewter allows uninvigilated exams at his place.
Avril conducts major surgery with no urge
to upgrade her status from nurse. L T Philpot lulls
the travelling enemy with safety, despite the neighbours & the
    Bible.
Hear us hail the Revolution; hear us toast our restraint!

Conversations at Upton Park *iv*

Like the story of the child on his first real train
who points out GENTLEMEN on station after station,
discovering that places have the same name:
that's why it fascinates him, this late in the day,
visiting his mother, who, as a treat, takes him back
to college which ruined a friend, and pins on him
a reminder of profession he wouldn't think to claim. And, yes,
he recognizes this as his own.

And in this room where Anancy stories are retold,
the two review a history, this volume subtitled
KNOWN, TOO, AT THIS ADDRESS, her place, his place, the same
station on the train. When they broke into his house
and robbed another, didn't he fail like a bad watchdog
those strangers who invited him to live amongst them?

Downstairs

They tell the story of a man, like Bobo,
painting a house in England. So there he is
outside on a bright day – you get the sun
in London, too, our people've been there, they know –
this man kneeling on a cushion painting the railings.
And – wait for it – he's wearing gloves!
So the housepainter, a worker, earns a cushion to kneel on
and gloves to keep him free of paint.

You might quibble now and say the gloves
were on different hands, a woman's washing up.
But downstairs they begin to see cushion and glove
not as decoration for the privileged at church
but something to protect them from discomfort
day in day out: so how do you translate *cushion* and *glove*?

The Writer Naming His Character

I'm not God, he thinks, I can't afford
to get it wrong and consume them in theology.
Or have them say: it doesn't quite fit
to call the elder brother of that family
with pretensions to learning – but no colour-
coding to their advantage – *Richard* (pencilled in)
to be converted Dick years later in England.
He would call him Eugene. The rightness of *Eugene*

that hint of a French play, smatterings
of *n'est-ce pas?* in the dialogue, his sister Avril
having someone to misquote Marivaux with
in the drawing-room at Coderington; dreams
of study at Montpellier more poignant now
with the decades of displacement in England written differently.

Needless

Needless, he say: 'Needless to say . . . '
our Philosopher who vied with Confucius &
Socrates for finesse. Or, when the mood changed
Hodgie was 'that Jackarse, that Clown'
for challenging us to take things literally.
Not satisfied with one linguistic coup
he dribbled pearls like: 'In other words . . . '
followed by words in no way related to 'in other words'.

Like my mother nearly said: 'Jam tomorrow and Jam yesterday
but no damn Jam today.' In other words: 'Meet me in Nairobi.'
Or: 'The Autobiography of Bertrand Russell'. Or even:
'Ya ni panimayu pa-ruski, I spit in your eye, I wish you dandruff.'
(O, let not the wise man glory in his wisdom.)
Needless to say . . . not exactly Socrates playing football.

Detail

That was the boy from Coderington, Stapleton
who threw up his studies and went off
not to Africa as they thought, but to New Guinea –
Papua New Guinea, that is – to create the media:
that's where he learnt Melanesian Pidgin,
Lukim yu & *bagarap* & *LongLong* & *SingSing*
underlining letters and postcards; that's the one.
But things have changed.

       'Lord' Balham at home
Mister Detail, if ever there was one
with his *William* Grant and *Gennady* Gerasimov etc.
has struck the counter-culture of broad brush
where countries are Third World, men abuse women,
we're all going to die and inherit feet of clay
and two plus two equals four, except when the fascist says so.

Each Day is the First Day
of the Rest of Our Lives

My steppes, O America, first sight
of Pyramids – the expanse
of Essequibo – and here she is
on the far bank, like a woman. First
of her race. Ah ha! She puts water bottle
to lips, drinks clean, quenches mine, drinks again.
Oh, this is no little war, my friend.

Remember when we sang, marched
off younger than the parents,
and put some miles – a century's
worth, let's say – between us and the cynics?
She had our children, we ruled
the country from afar. (Ah! and the songs.)
Not just another war, my friend.

A Sermon in the Basement

For there's always going to be a preacher in this family
to give us a fix. Eugene's boy, they say, is reading up on the Koran,
but that's for the next generation to sort out;
so, still, we congregate for the Castine once a year
at basecamp which we can't, as yet, abandon.
Here, in our cell – you call us terrorists? – we relearn
names from the house lost in travel: *family*, again, braced
against the hurricane of exile; even the parents brought back.

The Castine sheds the cloak of conman, an island boy
with little to offer except letters behind his name.
He comes, he reminds us, as in the old days, to sup at the table.
For despite collapse around us, and falling among thieves,
we carry the promise – in boasts and regrets – of the riches of home.
For, despite this space, we are not poor, not tired; we're nobody's
    huddled masses.

VIII

And After All That, a Love Poem

A curtain of black cloth covers the square
(a square like Tiananmen): we can't look down on it;
underneath – who knows? We know – what's going on?
The courage of last night seems an age away.
Today, the square is swept, is washed, and rents
in the concrete ill-speak that nothing happened.

And now here, in this place you can't pronounce,
they watch placid, eyes that have seen the worst.
The curtain is blue, is green of paradise, is stitched
with birdsong for there are no witnesses.
Those who have seen the worst would today be surprised
though we don't know it: is it luck

to light on survivors straggling out the morning after?
Who's this one – she won't now mind about children
nor miss the ease of early forms of speech; but of course
will wonder at ticks of life dear to her admirers:
she won't mind living that extra day or night
if rioters marauding through the body pause for breath.

And now to my torch in the night, my towrope,
your full set of teeth, good working limbs, etc.;
you who might draw this bile like a magic curtain
to reveal – see? – no scars: us, alive at an earlier time . . .
that lost instrument retuning with the band . . .
This trifle is for you, girl, another song, unaccompanied.

New and Recent Poetry from Anvil

HEATHER BUCK
Psyche Unbound

TONY CONNOR
Metamorphic Adventures

PETER DALE
Edge to Edge
NEW AND SELECTED POEMS

DICK DAVIS
Touchwood

CAROL ANN DUFFY (ed.)
Anvil New Poets 2

HARRY GUEST
Coming to Terms

MICHAEL HAMBURGER
Collected Poems 1941–1994

ANTHONY HOWELL
First Time in Japan

PETER LEVI
The Rags of Time

CHARLES MADGE
Of Love, Time and Places
SELECTED POEMS

DENNIS O'DRISCOLL
Long Story Short

PHILIP SHERRARD
In the Sign of the Rainbow
SELECTED POEMS 1940–1989

RUTH SILCOCK
A Wonderful View of the Sea

A catalogue of our publications is available on request